MEMORIES
OF OLD
LANCASHIRE

MEMORIES
OF OLD
LANCASHIRE

AURORA PUBLISHING

First published in Great Britain in 1994 by
Aurora Publishing
Unit 9 Bradley Fold Trading Estate
Radcliffe Moor Road, Bradley Fold
Bolton, Lancashire BL2 6RT

ISBN 1 85926 045 4 Hardback
ISBN 1 85926 047 0 Paperback

Produced by
PDH Book Print Production
Castleton, Rochdale OL11 2XD

Printed in Italy by:
- Tipografia Umbra -
Città di Castello

CONTENTS

LANCASHIRE

Lancashire has long been an area of contrasts. To the west, are the coastal resorts with Blackpool still reigning supreme for entertainment, day trips and holidays (no longer generally confined to Wakes weeks). Further inland is the supreme beauty of the Forest of Bowland with its rural villages and small market towns, culminating in the magical delights of Pendle Forest which has never managed to shake off its air of mystery and witchcraft from the 17th century. Indeed, anyone seeing the brooding magnificence of Pendle Hill automatically thinks of the days of superstition, spells and witch trials.

Moving south the industrial towns are reached, and eventually the great city of Manchester. Preston merits here a chapter of its own for the Preston Guilds which occur around every twenty years. Many of the towns are examples of the cotton, wool and cloth industries on which Lancashire was once prosperous. The Lancashire people, many stuck daily in their mills, were known to work hard and play hard. They enjoyed their small amount of leisure time to the full. The area is renowned for its Whit walks and Brass Bands and the spirit of bygone times is captured through these photographs.

Many Lancastrians believe that Lancashire is a county under-rated by others, perhaps partly because it stands next to Yorkshire with its stunning scenery, rich history and pleasant coastline. This is probably true and mainly stems from the fact that people from outside the area do not really know Lancashire. It still. has the reputation of dark satanic mills, dreary housing and poverty. These photographs show that Lancashire in times past is not all as the stereotype allows, and modern-day Lancashire is, of course, changing steadily, and is known today for its enterprise and culture more than its black pudding!

BY THE SEASIDE

Blackpool developed world fame with its Golden Mile of sand, its 6 miles of promenade and the spectacular annual illuminations. The 518 foot tower keeps a watchful eye over the town. It was the arrival of the railway in 1846 which brought industrial workers from all parts of Lancashire to the town for the Wakes Week holidays and the Victorian style entertainment. Now people come from throughout the UK and abroad to use its ultra modern facilities. The beach is said to be polluted, the streets are crowded and commercialism reigns supreme but there is still something peculiarly attractive about Blackpool, despite its lack of elegance. It is said to be the most fun of all the seaside resorts.

North Pier, Blackpool. c. 1936

A busy North Pier where the orchestra would play twice daily performances. A sunny day with some brisk walking going on and trams which would conveniently drop passengers at the Pier. This pier opened in 1863. Pier decks offered various amusements such as bands. Remaining piers are now often hailed as fine examples of Victorian and Edwardian architecture.

Aircraft on the Beach, Blackpool. c. 1915

Not a common sight these days, although there is a small airport on the outskirts of the town near to South Shore. The spacious, flat sandy beach would presumably be ideal for landing an aircraft. Now children watch them as tourists take flights over the sea, and some crossings to Ireland are made. This Avro 'plane would have been based in Manchester.

Launching the Lifeboat, Blackpool. c. 1932

The brave locals who went out in the boats were often in danger of perishing themselves. Lifeboats are now more sophisticated vessels, designed for buoyancy and for carrying advanced safety equipment. Here, the sea looks calm, and it is probably a less dramatic rescue that they were being called upon to do, but essential none the less.

Launching the Lifeboat, Fleetwood. c. 1916

The crowds gathered to watch the launch of the lifeboat, including the policeman. Many would be onlookers, but the families of the men would also doubtless be there. The RNLI was founded in 1824 in an attempt to preserve lives from shipwrecks. That aim has not changed, and the lifeboat service is an essential part of coastal life.

Midland Hotel, Morecambe. c. 1925

Morecambe is another of the popular Lancashire resorts. It never really managed to compete with Blackpool, but had the added advantage of superb sunsets across Morecambe Bay, a vast area of dangerous sand flat and shallows, dependent on the tides, and views to the hills of the Lake District beyond.

Ship Leaving Fleetwood. c. 1925

Fleetwood was a shipping port with a town and market developed away from the docks, but it somehow never achieved the importance of Liverpool. Some ships would leave from here to visit the Isle of Man, but mainly it developed as a deep sea fishing area. Seeing a ship leave is always a wonderful sight and a small crowd was attracted here despite the rain.

Central Pier Fire, Morecambe, 31st July, 1933

A dramatic photograph of smoke billowing from the fire on the
central pier. Piers were originally to allow disembarkation at high or
low tide, but soon became attractions in themselves. Fires at piers
seem to have been quite common.

Chiropodist on Morecambe Beach. c. 1920

It seems a peculiar way to spend your time on the beach but perhaps the salt water had a beneficial effect. Unlike the modern day health professionals whom we expect to see in clean, efficient surgeries, this chiropodist plied his trade on the beach, and obviously got some willing customers. Perhaps having one's corns pared while surveying the scene was a relaxing way to spend some time and all part of returning from the holiday refreshed!

Cliffs and Boating Pool, North Shore, Blackpool

Open Air Baths, South Shore, Blackpool

New Promenade, Blackpool. 1910

Now the visitors are often more likely to be seen in the plentiful amusement arcades and funfair rather than promenading by the sea-front. Promenading seems to have remained a continental habit but has lost popularity in Britain. Not an ideal occupation at bright and breezy Blackpool when it would be hard work to keep one's hat on!

Rough Sea at Blackpool. c. 1921

Every postcard seller has the now obligatory picture of rough seas at Blackpool. But the scene is certainly dramatic when the beach is cordoned off and the waves thrash onto the road. Sadly, lives have been lost when the sea has been in such an angry mood, of fishermen and also tourists, local people and animals just getting too close and being swept away by the waves.

SCENES FROM STREET LIFE

It is pictures of street life, which often bring the past back into focus. There are many photographs around of momentous occasions and national events, but the photographs taken by ordinary people, of normal life often tell us much more about the local history of an area. History has traditionally concentrated on events of great importance, but the re-discovery of everyday life is now considered to give a good deal of additional insight into the lives of our ancestors – some will call it nostalgia, but alongside oral history techniques, pictures from the past are now being used to look at the day-to-day lives of the everyday people who were the fabric of Lancashire.

Bacon Seller, Haslingden. c. 1905

Up in the Rossendale Valley, a bacon seller trundles along the road with his cart and horse, presumably having plied his trade. Haslingden was a cotton town and the centre of the cotton waste industry. The fairly steep rows of terraces and high surrounding moorland produce a picture that doesn't quite fit with the meaning of Haslingden, "Valley of the Hazel Trees".

A clearer understanding of the history of the area can be obtained at the nearby museum in Helmshore. The Textile Museum is housed in an old mill, previously used for the manufacture of blankets. One interesting feature is an early 19th century water wheel which was not replaced by electric motors until 1954. This is either indicative of the efficiency of water power or the fact that certain technological advances had passed this area by.

The Stocks, Poulton-le-Fylde. c. 1911

Poulton used to be the major port in the area. The River Wyre provided a safe anchorage and supported a ship building industry. It is significant that the railway reached Poulton in 1840, some six years before Blackpool. The advent of the railway led directly to the decline of Poulton as it enabled the rapid development and expansion of Fleetwood as a port and a holiday resort. The photograph is probably specially posed rather than an authentic villain in the stocks.

Yorkshire Street, Rochdale. c. 1910

A busy scene where Yorkshire Street meets Lord Street, significant for
the array of shops present. These were the days of the specialist shop,
such as the hat shop which would have done quite a trade judging by
the fact that some kind of head covering seemed obligatory. Social
status or occupation is also indicated by the type and style of the hat.
Rochdale began to prosper as early as the first half of the 16th century
with the growth of domestic cloth manufacturing which enabled
St. Chad's Church to be rebuilt. It still has carved Tudor pews dating
from that time.

Tim Bobbin, alias John Collier, the 18th century Lancashire poet is
buried in the churchyard. However, Rochdale's two main claims to
fame are as the birthplace of Gracie Fields and the place where the
first successful co-operative was founded in 1844. The building in
Toad Lane which housed the Co-op, known as the Rochdale Pioneers,
is now a museum.

Elliott Street, Tyldesley. c. 1929

A lively street scene on the junction with High Street in Tyldesley
which was an old mill area. Varying degrees of wealth are apparent
in this picture, from the smartly dressed, clean boys on the right, to
the more ragged appearance of the girls on the left.

Stoney Brow, Tottington. c. 1909

A semi-rural street scene in the village of Tottington near Bury, which hasn't changed very much. Stoney Brow shows the junction of Harwood Road to the left, leading to Four Lane Ends and Harwood, and Turton Road to the right, leading to the village of Affetside and the reservoirs of North Bolton. The Printer's public house to the right of the picture, on Chapel Street, remained of the same name (although updated) until 1993 when it was developed into an Italian restaurant.

Lancaster Road, Preston. c. 1914

Preston was an important Lancashire town for cotton spinning, but also for engineering and the docks. It housed some imposing buildings as may be seen on the left of this photograph and was relatively prosperous.

Bare Village. c. 1940

Bare village is located just outside Morecambe and has largely missed the effects of both the growth and subsequent decline of the area as a tourist attraction.

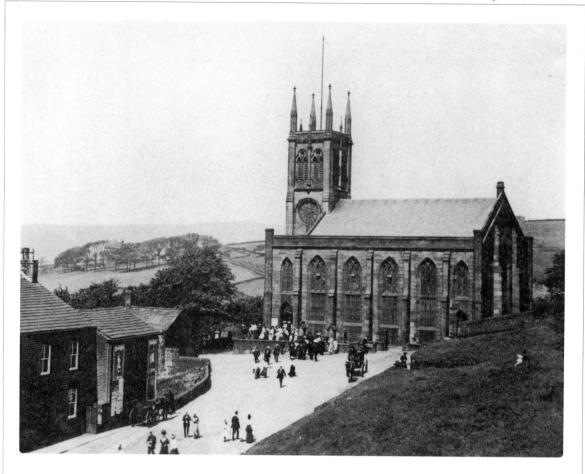

Saddleworth Church. c. 1910

A clear view of Saddleworth Church on a fine Sunday afternoon. Saddleworth is an area near to Oldham on the edge of brooding moorland which is the view in the distance.

Unfortunately, the area is now famous as the scene of the infamous Moors murders. which sadly overshadows the attractions of the town and its surrounding hills.

Wallgate, Wigan. c. 1930

A busy shopping street in Wigan. The policemen who are
presumably directing the traffic look a little redundant. Wigan can
easily trace its roots back to Roman times and is thought to be the site
of Coccium. The Borough of Wigan was also represented at Edward
I's Model Parliament in 1296, showing its importance before the
Industrial Revolution. Wigan's 19th century growth was based on
both cotton and coal. Wigan Pier is now a major tourist attraction.

Harehill Road, Littleborough. c. 1910

Littleborough was a cotton manufacturing town with a number of weavers' cottages. No transport in this picture but visible indications of use of horse-power on the cobbled road. Numbers of children seemed to congregate on this street.

Waterside, Colne. c. 1924

A tranquil scene in this cotton manufacturing town situated at the River Calder.

Church Street, Blackburn. c. 1907

A lively scene from this textile town with mill chimneys visible in the distance. Blackburn has avoided the worst effects of its decline in the Lancashire textile industry in the 20th century because it has been able to diversify. Engineering, manufacture of electrical equipment and brewing are all now major industries in Blackburn. The football club has had a dramatic resurgence in recent years after a long period of decline. There are unlikely to be many who can remember the last time they were top of the league at the end of the season. Here, a good deal of activity with traders, horses and carts and a few trams. The bobby on the beat was a common sight.

Wilpshire. c. 1911

There are not many photographs around of Wilpshire, the grand
sounding place which is in fact a small spot on the map between
Blackburn and Clitheroe. More developed today, but still an area of
some select housing, this photograph shows women buying produce
before the cart proceeds up the hill.

Rock Street, Bury. c. 1928

Now known as The Rock, the street has seen dramatic changes. The
town itself is noted as Lancashire's centre for black-pudding
production, a local delicacy made from freshly slaughtered cow or
pig blood with added fat and cereal. This is formed into a kind of
sausage and is often served as part of the traditional English breakfast.

Clitheroe Castle. c. 1908

Not greatly changed, a peaceful view of Clitheroe, the most northern
of Lancashire cotton towns and gateway to the Trough of Bowland
with its beautiful villages like Slaidburn and Waddington. Clitheroe
is the main market town of the Ribble Valley. The shell of the castle is
Norman, and prominent on its limestone knoll above the town, which
gives a marvellous view of the surrounding area. There are two
legends surrounding the castle – firstly that the large hole in the East
wall of the keep was caused by a cannon ball when Oliver Cromwell
attacked it; the second, and even harder to prove, that the devil threw
a rock at it from Pendle Hill.

Heysham Village. c. 1905

A splendid photograph of a smithy at work shoeing a horse, and a
group of children apparently posing for the photographer. Heysham
village has not changed much since this photograph. St Peter's
Church and the ruined St Patrick's Chapel may still be seen,
alongside coffins cut directly into the rock. Outside Heysham village,
the changes of the 20th century are obvious. The port has regular
sailings to the Isle of Man and the nuclear power station is an
unmistakeable sight. A further development may be seen out in
Morecambe Bay, the exploitation of a gas field.

THE INDUSTRIAL FACE OF LANCASHIRE

Lancashire, although an area of history and great beauty in parts, is mainly noted for its industrial heritage and landscape. Most Lancashire towns are associated with the cotton industry and have the remnants of the old cotton mills as testimony to the days when cotton was King! However, Lancashire also had engineering workshops, a number of coal mines, the Leyland Motor Works and other local industries. Although parts of Lancashire have declined, where old industries have collapsed, and the days of mass employment in the mills have long since gone, parts of the county remain commercially successful.

Winding Shop, Aqueduct Mill, Preston, c. 1905

Women workers in the winding shop where cotton production was in progress. Presumably, the winding shops were the original source of the children's Lancashire rhyme "Wind the Bobbin Up" still sung by young children today. As early as 1835, Preston had forty factories, primarily concerned with cotton spinning yielding 70,000 lbs of yarn per week.

Entrance to Leyland Motor Works, Leyland. c. 1920

The factory gates at "clocking off" time. Employees at Leyland Motors were fortunate between the Wars to be working in an industry which did not feel the recession of the 1930s as much as the more established textile factories. After World War II, Leyland Motors continued to thrive, developing a worldwide reputation for their buses and trucks. Sadly, the British car industry is now a mere shadow of its former glorious past.

A Leyland bus

Royal Visit to Trafford Park. c. 1903

The industrial arch to Trafford Park. Crowds thronging the area,
celebrating trade, and awaiting the excitement of a royal visit.

Fire Station, Rawtenstall. c. 1904

The then new fire station, erected 1897, in the Rossendale Valley's Rawtenstall. Now the old fire station, this functional and elegant building illustrates both a concern for the problems of fire fighting and a marked degree of civic pride. It was not until 1938 that it became compulsory for local authorities to have fire brigades.

Interior of Engineering Workshop. c. 1914

A packed engineering workshop at lunch time. A number of the men
are clutching their newspapers, some clad in overalls, others in
ordinary day wear, posing for this photograph. Notice all the
machinery is belt driven from shafts running under the ceiling. These
shafts were most likely turned by steam power. The working
conditions would not be allowable today due to extensive health and
safety legislation; in particular, the unguarded moving belts, clothing
hanging on work benches, poor lighting, overcrowding and noise.

Clitheroe Advertiser Printers, Clitheroe. c. 1913

Printers and their apprentices posing for a photograph, proudly showing the fruits of their labour, the "Clitheroe Advertiser". Provincial newspapers were growing dramatically at this time.

Clitheroe was the most northerly of the Lancashire cotton towns but never depended on a single source for its prosperity. Under the shadow of the Norman castle, the town, granted its first charter in the 12th century, continues to flourish.

Coach Builder, Accrington. c. 1921

In days still fairly heavily reliant upon horse drawn transport, the coach builder and wheelwright was an important local tradesman, shortly to become less necessary as motorisation grew in popularity.

Perhaps the state of the yard in this photograph shows that the wheelwright was already in serious economic decline. Accrington was incorporated as a town only in 1878 but it must have been substantially before that when it last reflected the meaning of its name, "village where acorns grow".

Burnt Mill, Barnoldswick. c. 1920

Concerned families, for whom this mill perhaps provided their
livelihood, stand surveying the scene of the burnt out shell of the mill.
The power of fire engines in the early years of the century would
have little chance of defeating a fire once it had become established in
a mill. The economic consequence would hit the whole community
due to unemployment and falling incomes until the mill could be
rebuilt.

Recruiting for Kitchener's Army, Albraham Picture Palace, Barnoldswick

Kitchener was appointed War Minister on the outbreak of World War I after a successful career during the Boer War. He later drowned (1916) when his ship was sunk on the way to Russia. He helped to modernise the British forces. Local buildings were often used for recruitment into the forces. It was considered a man's duty to sign up, though it was only later realised what hell many of them had in store. The Albraham Picture Palace was later completely destroyed by fire.

Laundry, Accrington. c. 1909

This picture speaks for itself really. Laundry work was considered women's work, and here the workforce are involved mainly in pressing the items. It must have been laborious, and tedious work, perhaps expressed by the faces of the women who look very solemn (although most photographs of people taken around this time are similarly unsmiling).

Oswaldtwistle Colliery Companies, no. 1 Rescue Team. c. 1906

The mine rescue team wearing self-contained oxygen breathing apparatus. The oxygen bottle would be at the back, and there would be a face mask for breathing it in. The rescuer would then exhale into the "sack" at the front, which would contain a filter and would make the oxygen re-usable. The equipment would last for around two hours of hard rescue work, but could be made to last much longer if necessary. The high number of accidents in mines would put these men in demand.

MARKET DAYS AND TOWN CENTRES

Busy market scenes and main streets are always cheering, when town centres appeared to be a hive of activity. Sadly, a number of markets no longer function as they used to, but some are still thriving, such as Tommyfield Market in Oldham. Market towns prospered in the Middle Ages but most are now in decline with the markets a shadow of their former selves.

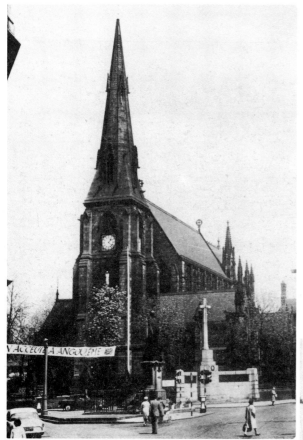

Parish Church and War Memorial, Bury

Although the buildings in towns may remain as they were years ago, the increased pressure on road space caused by the motor car has led to many changes in road layout. Nearly all towns have schemes designed to restrict access and keep traffic away from the centres, measures which are apparent in both Bury and Nelson.

The Centre, Nelson

Tommyfield Market, Oldham. c. 1915

Tommyfield Market is still in existence today though changes have been made. The mill chimneys of this cotton spinning town are highly visible in the background. While the shawls remind us of earlier days, they were probably worn for warmth as Oldham is one of the highest towns in the country.

Ormskirk Market. c. 1906

The market town of Ormskirk, surrounded by agricultural land but reasonably close to Preston and Liverpool. Ormskirk was well known for its gingerbread which would doubtless be sold on this market. Agriculture in the Ormskirk area also benefited greatly from the proximity of the Leeds-Liverpool canal which brought large quantities of night-soil from the industrial conurbations.

Town Hall and Memorial Garden, Rochdale

Market Place, Oldham

Market Street, Manchester. c. 1922

Manchester was the old cotton capital of Britain. This picture shows a crowded scene in Market Street including a close-up view of a tram going from Albert Square to Palatine Road, bowler hatted gents, policemen and horse-drawn transport.

Market Square, Wigan. c. 1908

The old Market Hall and the outdoor market in the square at Wigan
with various traders selling their goods.

THE COMMERCIAL HEART

The pictures of some of the small traders which were dotted around Lancashire are included, partly because so many of them have disappeared with the advent of huge supermarkets and out of town shopping. Some are still to be found – most towns have a number of fish and chip shops, for example, but the sight of a black pea seller with his cart has now disappeared for ever. Those shops which do still exist, such as shoe menders now tend to be part of a nationwide chain of shops, so the uniqueness of different shops is disappearing. Perhaps consumer sovereignty rules, where people want cheaper goods, preferably under one roof. Shopping no longer seems to be such a social occasion when shops were a vital part of local communities – although town centres do still tend to be meeting places. Whether to the good or not, shopping styles have changed.

Bicycle Stall, Accrington Market. c. 1905

The wonderful sight of a market stall crammed with bicycles: ladies
cycles, secondhand bikes, racer cycles. Oh, for the days when a good
racing cycle cost around £12. 00. The stall holders looked very smart,
and were obviously dressed to sell!

Black Pea Seller, Accrington. c. 1921

Once a common sight on the streets of Lancashire, the black pea seller is now generally obsolete except at fairs and celebrations, though black peas are still widely available in greengrocers throughout Lancashire. For a few pennies, children in particular, would delight in a cup full of black peas, usually soaked overnight, cooked, and served in vinegar and eaten with a spoon. Now, presumably, there would be little profit to be made and not enough people on the streets to make black pea selling profitable. Now, people devour them with a sense of nostalgia at fairgrounds and bonfires where they are a nutritious, warming snack.

Boot & Shoe Repairer, Oldham. c. 1910

This particular shoe repairer was Mr. J. Leonard of 178, Heron Street, Hollinwood, Oldham. Such a specialist shop would be unlikely to survive in today's competitive market where shoe repairers tend to be members of large chains of shops, or are quite often a sideline to some other more lucrative business. The throw away culture of today, and the availability of cheaper products, along with rapidly changing fashions, perhaps means that shoes are repaired less often than in the past.

Miller's Cafe, Belle Vue. 1926

This photo was taken in the days when Belle Vue was quite a local attraction as the posters on the wall show offering a zoo, fireworks, dancing and skating. Belle Vue was where Maggie Hobson and Will Mossop spent their day's honeymoon outing in the novel "Hobson's Choice". Now scarcely recognisable, Belle Vue is an inner city area needing regeneration with the zoo long since gone.

Market Hall, Bury. c. 1929

The old Market Hall, sadly no longer in existence in Bury. Bury is still well known for its market, but it has shifted to another part of town. Bury Black Puddings are still made and sold on the market.

Ironmongery Store, Ormskirk. c. 1903

One of those wonderful ironmongery stores which seem to be disappearing rapidly but which appeared to stock almost everything from wool to cleaning brushes, mats and linoleum to mops and shopping baskets. Now the tendency is towards specialisation rather than a convenient collection of useful small items which people need.

Fish and Chip shop, Oldham. c. 1910

The great British, and particularly northern institution, the Fish and Chip shop offering the staple Friday fare to many local families of fish, chips and peas, and generally, in Lancashire, gravy, wrapped in newspaper (now more hygienic white paper and more likely to include delicacies like spring rolls, curry sauce, etc). A convenience food, it has been popular with the British for over a hundred years, and seems to be one type of shop which has not disappeared from our streets. This particular chippy was J.F. Smith of 4, Bar Gap Road, Oldham.

CHILDREN AT PLAY

This section contains some interesting pictures of children at leisure. Interesting because there is a lot of publicity in modern times about children left to play by themselves on the streets, and some nostalgia about how it used to be. A number of the pictures here show children playing by themselves, apparently unsupervised by adults in many instances, with the very young cared for by the older children. Were times any safer for children then? Many of the pictures pre-date the widespread use of the motor car and certainly cars travelling at speed, so playing on the streets was in one respect undoubtedly safer. Perhaps nostalgia for the safe old days is simply that?

Punch and Judy Show, Morecambe. c. 1920

Punch and Judy is a traditional puppet show, now mainly confined to occasional appearances at the seaside. It is full of beating and fighting by Punch who epitomises the brutal husband. He is merciless to his wife and eventually kills her and other victims, including the baby who is usually thrown out of the window. There are shadows of earlier mystery plays where Punch always meets his doom – so, despite the violence, it is a moral tale.

Old Punch, Blackpool. c. 1930

The once popular pastime of Punch and Judy, common as
entertainment on the beaches for children. In this particular
show is a dog, Toby, (always a real dog) who would sit at the
side of the booth throughout the performance. There may have
been a reason for this, or he may simply have provided
additional entertainment.

Children's Corner, Morecambe. c. 1914

In the days when Morecambe's sands
were thronged with visitors.
Lots of children paddling in the
shallows, watched by their parents,
many wearing cumbersome dresses
and confined to the sands.

Beach & Pier, St. Annes-on-Sea. c. 1914

St. Annes held many attractions for children such as bathing, sailing, and playing on the sandy beaches. Here are children with their fishing nets and their buckets and spades having a wonderful time. How cumbersome the clothes looked however, for playing in the water, especially the dresses of the girls.

New Council School, Accrington. c. 1921

By now, young children were well out of the workforce and were required to attend school. This was a period of great school building around the country. Most youngsters would still leave school at 14 to go into an apprenticeship, and the degree of education they received was generally elementary in nature. It was not until the 1944 Education Act that children received universal, free State secondary education.

Carry Bridge, Colne. c. 1914

A semi-rural picture with children playing at the roadside.

Boating Lake, St. Annes-on-Sea. c. 1925

More fun at the seaside, this time at the boating lake, rather more serene and skilful entertainment than paddling!

DIDN'T WE HAVE
A LOVELY TIME?

Lancashire folk were known for their hard labour as they worked to make ends meet. They were also renowned for their ability to enjoy their leisure time to the full. Chapter one already illustrates the fun that people had at places like Blackpool, but other more day-to-day entertainment also occurred outside the home: the theatre, the afternoon brass bands in the parks, football, and outdoor walks. The old Whitsun Walks were quite an occasion and were often held alongside May fairs, feasts and village parties.

Whitsun Walks, Wrightington Bar. c. 1929

1920s costumes abound for this Whitsun Walk, held by St. James
Sunday School. The Whit Walks were once a popular event held
throughout Lancashire, but seem to have died out now.

Carnival Procession in Chorley

Grand Old Tyme Festival, Wesleyan Church, Prestwich

Theatre Royal, Bury. c. 1920

The old Theatre Royal no longer exists, indeed Bury no longer has a
theatre. Most small Lancashire towns no longer host theatres,
unfortunately. Along with many other of its more interesting
buildings, the loss of the Theatre Royal has left Bury with an
uninspiring town centre

Last Mile Road, Pendle. c. 1906

Pendle is renowned for its 17th century tales of witchcraft, the surrounding villages the home of characters with lovely names like Old Demdike, Old Chattox and Alice Nutter. The story of the witches still fascinates, but Pendle is also an area of spectacular moorland and meadow. Pendle Hill gives a marvellous view from the summit. It stands 1,832 feet above sea level and is seven miles long. In the past, Pendle was one of a chain of beacons used to summons the local yeomen to arms, as it was visible from all the surrounding areas. It has been the home to Roman legions, Norman invaders and Christian missionaries preaching to the pagans.

Bandstand, Heaton Park, Manchester. c. 1925

Rarely so crowded these days, Heaton Park boasts 600 acres of land, but the bandstand is no longer used. The Sunday afternoon bands during Summer days were popular, as is obvious from the crowds on this photograph. The huge park was also ideal promenading territory for a walk in the fresh air of north Manchester.

Albraham Picture House Fire, Barnoldswick

The Albraham Picture House is featured earlier (p. 36) as a recruitment centre for Kitchener's Army. Here, interested onlookers, mainly children, investigate the charred remains.

Sunday School Parade, Oldham. c. 1928

The Methodist Sunday School Parade, on Rochdale Road, Oldham. The Lancashire towns were renowned for their brass bands and these would often be on display leading the Sunday School parades. Usually, the parades would attract crowds of followers as they marched through the streets, and a number of onlookers. While Sunday Schools are now voluntary classes to provide children with basic instruction in Christianity, in the early days they were also an attempt to combat illiteracy among the poor.

Yachts in harbour, Hollingworth
Lake, Littleborough

The famous Besses o' th' Barn Band

Bolton Wanderers Football Team, 1920–21

The game of football, or soccer, is said to be southern in origin, but
soon came to be dominated by the working-class northern clubs. Here
we have the Wanderers, Bolton's team, shortly after the end of World
War I.

Llewellyn Railway, Southport. c. 1918

BYGONE TRANSPORT

Back to the days of steam engines, trams, the heyday of the railways and use of the canals for industrial transportation – all far removed from today's motorways, lorries and millions of cars. Lancashire is now pretty much divided by motorways, and includes two of the busier ones, the M6 and the M62. No longer are the old forms of transport suitable for the speed and high degree of activity of modern life. However, these photographs bring back reminiscences of a slower pace of life.

London Road Station, Manchester. c. 1914

Now the site of Piccadilly Station for all routes south, the scene is still recognisable despite changes to buildings. Taxis now amass in the area where the horse drawn carriages are in this photograph.

Barton Bridge. c. 1924

A swing bridge which was later to cause traffic queues whenever it was swung.

Nos. 6, 7, & 8 Docks, Trafford Wharf, Manchester

Docks 6–8 were for ocean-going ships and were constructed on the western side of Trafford Road. Sadly, the Manchester Ship Canal is no longer of great importance to the area; most freight now travels by road or rail to the ports. The Ship Canal was originally hailed as one of the greatest Victorian engineering achievements, and offered a trade advantage to industrial Lancashire by cutting freight charges. The area surrounding the docks in this photograph contained workers' terraced housing, mills and factories. There have been some changes but the area is still primarily that of working class, industrial Manchester.

Wigan Pier. c. 1914

The pier is now mainly used as a tourist attraction and has been regenerated. The book, "The Road to Wigan Pier" by George Orwell actually refers to a wharf on the Leeds and Liverpool Canal.

H. Viney & Co. Ltd. Preston. c. 1907

A steam lorry carrying sacks and barrels in Preston.

Town Centre, Bury

Passengers boarding the No. 9 bus to Jericho.

THE PRESTON GUILDS

Held every 20 years, the Preston guilds are of historic interest but also still take place, so are of contemporary relevance, too. These photographs are all taken from the 1922 guild and illustrate some of the numerous activities taking place.
A guild is thought to have existed in Saxon times in Preston, but the first procession is thought to have taken place around 1500. One of the most important aspects of the early guilds was the enrolling of freemen, so the guild rolls became records of the local population.
The guilds have been held regularly at 20 year intervals since 1542 apart from the 1942 guild which was postponed because of World War II. The mayor elected for a guild year is known as a guild mayor and the guild is celebrated by a three-day fair.
Some of the activities are encountered in the following pages.

The Women's Institute showing off their handicrafts

The WI was started as a means of providing classes in domestic science and homemaking, in an attempt to better educate women, especially in rural areas, in such matters. Selling home-produced goods and attempting to improve the quality of family life are now considered synonymous with the work of the WI.

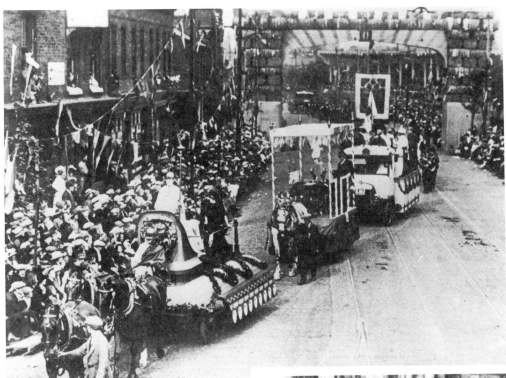

Arch of Bales

The Trades Procession going under the Arch of Bales. The Guilds were an opportunity for traders to maintain a float and advertise themselves.

Rushbearers

Rush-bearing survives in some English towns and villages, but is mainly a Lancastrian and Cumbrian tradition. Rushes were originally used to cover the cold, stone flagged floors of churches, which were renewed annually at a ceremony.

Queen Elizabeth goes to meet her petitioners. A role play enacting the days of the Virgin Queen

The role play probably celebrates the granting of the town's great charter by Elizabeth I in 1566, which ratified and extended all previous royal grants.

"Merrie England", with dancing around the maypole
Such activities were prohibited in Puritan times which must have
been a blow to Catholic Preston. The streamers or ribbons would be
woven into a complicated pattern by the dancers as they skipped
around the pole to celebrate the coming of Summer.

Morris Dancers
Teams of Morris dancers (following old Moorish traditions of
dancing) would folk dance throughout England, usually on May Day,
Whitsun, and early Summer.